Let's Talk About
SNOOPING

Grolier Enterprises Inc. offers a varied selection of both
adult and children's book racks. For details on ordering,
please write: Grolier Enterprises Inc., Sherman Turnpike,
Danbury, CT 06816 Attn: Premium Department

Let's Talk About
SNOOPING

By JOY BERRY

Illustrated by John Costanza
Edited by Orly Kelly
Designed by Jill Losson

GROLIER ENTERPRISES CORP.

Let's talk about SNOOPING.

When you get into people's things without their knowing about it or wanting you to, you are SNOOPING.

When you try to find things out about people without their knowing or wanting you to, you are SNOOPING.

SNOOPING is being nosy in a sneaky, meddlesome way.

No one likes it when someone snoops.

It is important that you treat other people the way you want to be treated.

If you do not want other people to snoop, you must not snoop.

It is important to *respect other people*. Do not listen secretly to what other people are saying. When other people are talking together, do not try to listen to their conversation without their knowing about it.

When someone is talking on the telephone,
do not listen in on another telephone.

Do not spy on other people.

Do not watch other people without their knowing it.

Do not pry into another person's business.

Do not try to learn things about people that they may not want you to know.

It is important to *respect other people's property.*

Do not look into the windows of people's houses without their knowing about it.
If the door is ajar, don't snoop.

Do not go into someone's room without asking. If the door to a room is closed, knock on it and wait to be invited before you go in.

Do not get into another person's dresser drawers, cupboards, or closets without permission.

Do not read things that have been written to another person unless the person says that you may.

It is important to *respect other people's privacy.*

It is OK for people to have thoughts and feelings that they keep to themselves.

Do not try to get people to share the thoughts and feelings that they may not want to share.

When you snoop, people may feel that they cannot depend on you. They may feel that they cannot trust you to be around them or their things.

Thus, snooping is not good for you, and it is not good for the people around you.

It is important to treat other people the way you want to be treated.

If you do not want other people to snoop, you must not snoop.